Goodbye, Iphigenia

A Play

George MacEwan Green

A Samuel French Acting Edition

FOUNDED 1830

SAMUELFRENCH-LONDON.CO.UK
SAMUELFRENCH.COM

Copyright © 1988 by George MacEwan Green
All Rights Reserved

GOODBYE, IPHIGENIA is fully protected under the copyright laws of the British Commonwealth, including Canada, the United States of America, and all other countries of the Copyright Union. All rights, including professional and amateur stage productions, recitation, lecturing, public reading, motion picture, radio broadcasting, television and the rights of translation into foreign languages are strictly reserved.

ISBN 978-0-573-12312-2

www.samuelfrench-london.co.uk

www.samuelfrench.com

FOR AMATEUR PRODUCTION ENQUIRIES

UNITED KINGDOM AND WORLD EXCLUDING NORTH AMERICA

plays@SamuelFrench-London.co.uk

020 7255 4302/01

Each title is subject to availability from Samuel French, depending upon country of performance.

CAUTION: Professional and amateur producers are hereby warned that GOODBYE, IPHIGENIA is subject to a licensing fee. Publication of this play does not imply availability for performance. Both amateurs and professionals considering a production are strongly advised to apply to the appropriate agent before starting rehearsals, advertising, or booking a theatre. A licensing fee must be paid whether the title is presented for charity or gain and whether or not admission is charged.

The professional rights in this play are controlled by Samuel French Ltd, 52 Fitzroy Street, London, W1T 5JR.

No one shall make any changes in this title for the purpose of production. No part of this book may be reproduced, stored in a retrieval system, or transmitted in any form, by any means, now known or yet to be invented, including mechanical, electronic, photocopying, recording, videotaping, or otherwise, without the prior written permission of the publisher. No one shall upload this title, or part of this title, to any social media websites.

The right of George MacEwan Green to be identified as author of this work has been asserted by him in accordance with Section 77 of the Copyright, Designs and Patents Act 1988

CHARACTERS

King Agamemnon, Commander of the Greek Armies at Aulis
Kalchas, the High Priest
Andreas, a young soldier
Queen Clytemnestra, wife of Agamemnon
Iphigenia, daughter of Agamemnon and Clytemnestra
Penelope, a young maid-servant to Iphigenia

The action takes place in a military camp in ancient Greece

GOODBYE, IPHIGENIA

A couch, carpets, and hangings arranged to convey the impression of the interior of a tent are UR. *An altar-shaped structure draped overall in black material is* UC

When the play opens both UR *and* UC *areas are in darkness*

A male figure, Andreas, dressed in a full-length cloak with a hood that completely conceals his face, enters L *and moves* DC. *He walks with the shuffling tread of an old man. As he comes forward, he is singing in a high, piping, tuneless voice*

Andreas (*singing*) Helen was a randy bitch,
Randy bitch, randy bitch,
When Paris came she got the itch,
Got the itch, got the itch.
She left 'er old man's 'ouse and bed
To join the whores o' Troy instead,
And for 'er sake you died and bled,
You silly bleeding soldiers.

(*Speaking*) Agh, those young ones, what do they know about any o' that? "Don't give us none o' that ancient 'istory, Dad," that's what the young folk say. Just try telling 'em something about it— give 'em a bit o' education, like—and all they can do is groan and say, "Ow, my God, 'e's off again". Ruddy ignorant little twerps. One o' 'em says, "Who the bleeding 'ell was that Helen, anyway?" and afore a body can give 'em a slither o' enlightenment, another one says, "Why the bleeding 'ell should anyone care!" I say, "She were just the most beautiful woman in the 'ole bleeding world, that's who she were". Then they say, "'ad she big tits, Dad? Nice piece o' bum, Dad?" I say, "She were a lady, a princess, wife to Menelaus who were brother o' King Agamemnon, that's who she were". They say, "But 'ad she big knockers, old Dad?" They do it to tease. I know that. Not such an old fool but I know that. Still, they should show some respect. Not for Helen necessarily. No, for she weren't no better than an 'igh-class tart, leaving Menelaus, 'er lawful 'usband and everything, and scarpering off to Troy wi' that poncy Prince Paris. All false curls, silk tunics, furs and jewels, 'e were. A right male tart if ever I clapped eyes on one.

No, but they should show respect for us—us wot was in the biggest Greek army the world 'as ever seen. That's a fact. It's in the 'istory books, 'nt it. All the kings and princes and toffs o' all the states o' the Greek federation formed an alliance to go to Troy to bring Helen back to 'er conjugal bed. Well, they 'ad to, 'adn't they? I mean, the attack on one prince's honour was tantamount to an attack on the 'ole bleeding lot o' 'em. Turn a blind eye on one case o' foreign seduction and who could tell whose turn it would be next. A thousand ships—no lie, a thousand bleeding ships—it took to convoy that army to Troy. So that shows you 'ow many o' us there was. Only we got stuck at the port o' Aulis. Bloody well becalmed we was. Not a single puff o' wind to stir the sails. And that's 'ow Iphigenia, poor cow, come into the picture. Iphigenia? You know, Princess Iphigenia, first daughter o' King Agamemnon, Commander in Chief o' the 'ole army, and his wife Queen Clytemnestra, who, by the by, were sister to Helen. They're all inter-married is toffs. Lot o' inbreeding goes on among 'em. Anyways, who do you think were on sentry-go outside the private and personal tent o' Queen Clytemnestra and Princess Iphigenia when they come to Aulis, eh? Go on, who do you think? (*He pulls back the hood of his cloak and throws the front of the cloak back over his shoulders, revealing himself now as a young man, dressed in a short tunic with a sheathed sword at his side. With a flourish, he unsheathes the sword and moves* UR)

Lights come up UR *on the interior of the tent. Andreas moves back*

Goodbye, Iphigenia

and forth a few times in military-like fashion, stamping his feet with some force, and then coming to a halt. Quietly and tunelessly he begins to sing

> Dear Ma, 'ere's a little note
> From your darling soldier boy.
> 'e's gorn to fight the frigging foe
> In the frigging land o' Troy.
> But, Ma, there ain't no ruddy boat
> That'll take your lad afloat
> To where 'e dearly longs to go.
> Oh, Ma, 'ow very, very foul is
> A soldier's life in Aulis,
> In rotten Aulis by the sea.
>> Oh, Ma, wot a bleeding 'ole,
>> Wot a bleeding 'ole
>> Is Aulis.
>> Oh, Ma, we're really up the pole,
>> Really up the pole,
>> In Aulis.

High Priest Kalchas enters L *and approaches Andreas*

Andreas comes to attention and raises his sword in salute

Kalchas Sentry, is King Agamemnon about?
Andreas No, sir, your reverence, I 'aven't seen 'im since I come on duty.
Kalchas I'll wait upon him in the tent.
Andreas As it please your Holiness, sir. (*He stands aside to let Kalchas pass by him*)

Kalchas sits upon the couch. Andreas relaxes his stance

> (*Singing very quietly*) Oh, Ma, we're really up the pole,
>> Really up the pole,
>> In Aulis.

King Agamemnon enters L and crosses the stage towards Andreas

Andreas snaps to attention

Agamemnon Has High Priest Kalchas been here, sentry?
Andreas Yes, Majesty, sir. 'E's waiting for Your Majesty inside, sir.

Agamemnon passes by Andreas to enter the tent area. At his entrance, Kalchas rises from the couch. Andreas moves slightly closer to the tent interior area, adopting the pose of one eavesdropping on what is being said within the tent

Agamemnon Ah, Kalchas, I've just come from a meeting—I mean, a meeting of the general staff.
Kalchas Yes, Your Majesty?
Agamemnon Yes. Well, we discussed—yes, discussed—this matter of Iphigenia—of my daughter, Iphigenia—at some length.
Kalchas Yes, Majesty?
Agamemnon Yes, we did, and the final decision—of the general staff, that is—was that I should approach you—that is, in your capacity of High Priest——
Kalchas It is the only capacity I have, sir.
Agamemnon What? Oh! Point taken. The thing is, it was decided I could—no, I mean, *should*—approach you to—to—seek—yes, seek—absolute assurance—that is, absolute confirmation—that there is no way—I mean, *absolutely* no way—of reversing your ruling about—well, you know, Iphigenia—my poor dear Iphigenia.
Kalchas Sire, it is hardly *my* ruling. It is a dictate from on high. Moreover, when it was presented to the general staff and yourself, it was unanimously agreed it should be obeyed.
Agamemnon Yes, yes, I know all that, but the thing is—well, dash it all, Kalchas, did we really, really comprehend the gravity of what was being proposed?
Kalchas For my part, Majesty, my comprehension was utterly complete. Are you saying, sire, that the general staff and yourself have had a change of heart?

Goodbye, Iphigenia 5

Agamemnon No, not exactly. Not a change of heart as such.
Kalchas Are you going back, sire, on the word you solemnly gave?
Agamemnon Certainly not! I rather resent that inference, Kalchas. What I mean is, surely there must be some alternative course—a compromise sort of thing.
Kalchas Majesty, you must realise that if true religion is to be upheld there can be no accommodation granted to compromise—not even, to use your phrase, "a compromise sort of thing".
Agamemnon But it is so damnably hard. So intolerably hard. Kalchas, I am a father.
Kalchas Exactly, sire, and not just a father to your own offsprings, but, as a king, you are the father of all your people. In the role of king you must act in the best interests of all your children, giving no preferential consideration to your own flesh and blood. However, sire, the decision whether or not to proceed in this matter rests entirely with you.
Agamemnon But not to proceed would mean——
Kalchas (*interrupting*) That the current situation would continue indefinitely. And, sire, time lost could mean a war lost. Then again, as far as the army is concerned, especially the rank and file, you would—not to put too fine a point on it——
Agamemnon (*interrupting*) I know, I know. I'd lose face.
Kalchas And authority, sire. You have already sent for the princess?
Agamemnon Yes. In fact, a messenger has just brought word that she and the Queen will be here presently.
Kalchas Brave young creature to come so meekly to meet her destiny.
Agamemnon Ah, that's the thing, Kalchas. She doesn't know—doesn't know exactly—why she's been summoned here.
Kalchas Oh, dear. But the Queen knows, doesn't she?
Agamemnon No, I could not risk telling Clytemnestra. I mean, she might have refused to bring Iphigenia. You know, Kalchas, what a mother's love can be like. I had to use subterfuge, don't you see?
Kalchas What form, sire, has this subterfuge taken?
Agamemnon (*quietly, shamefacedly*) I said I'd arranged a marriage.

Kalchas (*feigning difficulty of hearing*) Sorry, sire, I didn't quite catch that.
Agamemnon (*loudly, defiantly*) I said I'd arranged a marriage for Iphigenia.
Kalchas With whom?
Agamemnon I didn't specify. Naturally, they'd understand it would be to someone of high rank—a gentleman and hero.
Kalchas So Iphigenia thinks she is coming at her father's command to surrender her virginity upon the altar of marriage.
Agamemnon It was a necessary deception.
Kalchas A deception that will have to be revealed to her—and to her mother—as soon as they arrive.
Agamemnon Unless we can think of some other way——
Kalchas There is no other way. Not, that is, if we rule out the coward's way.
Agamemnon If only you knew how a father's heart bleeds.
Kalchas That it bleeds does you credit, I'm sure. But civic and military honour take precedence over private feelings and personal vulnerability.

From off stage comes the sound of trumpet fanfares merging with a cacophony of male voices raised in cheering and shouting

Agamemnon Oh, pitiless heaven, they've arrived in camp!
Kalchas It would certainly appear to be the case.
Agamemnon My child, my poor, poor child!
Kalchas Let us go to meet them.

Clytemnestra enters L, followed by Iphigenia and then Penelope

Agamemnon and Kalchas go towards C to meet them. Clytemnestra bobs a very slight curtsy and then kisses Agamemnon on the cheek

Clytemnestra Rough soldiery they may be, Agamemnon, but the language of your army as our chariots moved through the camp was quite, quite inexcusably disgusting. I am no prude, as you

Goodbye, Iphigenia 7

very well know, but I must say that on this occasion I was deeply shocked.
Agamemnon Why? What did they say, my dear?
Clytemnestra I do not care to repeat the things they shouted at us. Sufficient to say it had to do with the consummation of a marriage.
Agamemnon I'm sure you're mistaken, Clytemnestra. Everyone knows Iphigenia isn't going to be——

Kalchas interrupts with a warning cough. Agamemnon blusters

But come, my darling child, won't you come forward to greet your poor old dad?

Iphigenia steps towards Agamemnon, curtsies and then kisses him on both cheeks

Iphigenia I'm so happy, Majesty, to have been summoned to you here at Aulis.
Agamemnon My child, my dearest darling child. (*He takes Iphigenia into a close embrace and holds her there*)
Clytemnestra Iphigenia, you're such a sly-boots, you really are. (*To Kalchas*) She's like a hen dancing on a hot griddle, desperate to know who has been chosen to be her bridegroom. (*To Agamemnon*) I must confess, husband, I'm more than a shade inquisitive on that score myself. I'll tell you here and now I'll exercise my right as a mother to veto any unsuitable choice. I won't have my daughter forcibly hitched up to any pock-raddled, pot-bellied old buffoon, even should he be as rich as Croesus. I have quite a definite image of the man I should call son-in-law, and that certainly isn't someone even one day older than myself. How humiliating it would be to have an old man call one Mother. Now, for goodness sake, husband, release the child before you smother her quite to death. (*To Kalchas*) He ever spoiled her since the day I endured the agony of her birth. For all the size of her, it was the most excruciating experience of my life. But, there, what do you men know or care about the torment of child-bearing!

Agamemnon (*reluctantly releasing Iphigenia*) My darling little flower would never knowingly cause anyone a moment's pain. She is the most precious of all my possessions.
Iphigenia But soon, Daddy, to be possessed by another. Won't you please reveal to me his name?
Kalchas (*to Agamemnon*) Perhaps it would be circumspect, Majesty, to retire to the tent.
Clytemnestra Quite right, Kalchas. Here we are stuck out in the open in the full heat of day—not a circumstance conducive to maintaining a delicate complexion. It would not do to have a bride with skin as tough as tanned leather. We women are required to sacrifice a lot for the gratification of our men, but I firmly draw the line at sacrificing the delicacy of one's skin. Agamemnon and Iphigenia, lead on. (*To Penelope*) Girl, fetch the luggage from the chariot. (*To Andreas*) And you, young soldier, give her a hand. (*To Kalchas*) And from you, our dear High Priest, I beg the support of your arm.

Agamemnon puts his arm around Iphigenia's waist and leads her towards the UR *tent area, followed by Kalchas and Clytemnestra*

Andreas sheathes his sword and exits L *with Penelope*

When the four characters reach the tent interior, their area of the stage is plunged into darkness

Andreas and Penelope enter L, *carrying a trunk between them*

They set the trunk down C *and Andreas sits upon it*

Andreas So you're maidservant to Princess Iphigenia, is you?
Penelope Lady's maid is the job description I prefer, soldier.
Andreas Ooh, get you, Miss Big Ideas.
Penelope If you're into name-calling, I could think of quite a few for you.
Andreas Such as?

Goodbye, Iphigenia 9

Penelope Oh, let's see. Bumptious Bert. Private Pride. Mr Muscle Brain.
Andreas Miss Smart Mouth. (*He laughs*) Wot's your real name, sweetheart?
Penelope Not sweetheart, anyway. If you must know, it's Penelope.
Andreas Nice name. Classy sort o' moniker. Suits you.
Penelope From insult to compliment so quickly. A girl would be wise to be cautious when she's around you, Private Smoothie.
Andreas Andreas. The name's Andreas.
Penelope Andreas. Quite a nice name—in a masculine sort of way, I mean.
Andreas I'm masculine all right. Say it again.
Penelope What?
Andreas My name.
Penelope Why?
Andreas Go on.
Penelope Andreas. So what?
Andreas So I love the way you say it. It feels good when you say it.
Penelope That sounds like a well-used line to me.
Andreas No, it ain't. I swear it, Penelope.
Penelope Well, if you say so, Andreas.
Andreas Wot was the soldiers shouting at you when you come into camp?
Penelope Wasn't shouting at me. At my poor dear lady they was yelling, the loud-mouthed devils.
Andreas But wot?
Penelope Here, I'm not the sort of girl who'd repeat them sort of things.
Andreas Go on, no-one's listening but me.
Penelope W-e-ll, I can't hardly remember it all, but some cried out, "Don't worry, Princess darling, it won't 'urt when 'e sticks it into you". And some said, "When you're lying there, little one, and 'e does it to you, remember it's for Greece".
Andreas Yes, I can see 'ow that sort o' thing might be taken the wrong way. Wot did the princess say?
Penelope Oh, my princess is a perfect lady. Let on she hadn't heard

a blinking word. Well, to tell the truth, the Queen clapped her hands over my lady's ears. Anyway, Iphigenia wouldn't have paid it too much mind, for all she can think about is who her father has chosen to be her husband. I expect they're telling her that right now.
Andreas Well, they're telling 'er something.
Penelope Ooh, Andreas, I wonder what his name is.

From the darkness of the UR *area come a series of female screams and hysterical sobbing*

Andreas (*rising from the trunk*) I reckon as they've told 'er.

Penelope, in alarm, moves close to Andreas and allows him to put his arms around her in a gesture of comforting

Penelope Blessed heaven, what have they told her?
Andreas They've told 'er, Penelope girl, that 'is name is death.
Penelope What does that mean? What kind of silly talk is that?

Clytemnestra, in obvious fury, rushes from the darkened UR *area. Kalchas comes at her heels. Andreas releases Penelope from his embrace*

What do you mean—death?
Andreas Take an end o' the trunk and I'll tell you over yonder.

Andreas and Penelope pick up the trunk and carry it R *just as Clytemnestra and Kalchas arrive* C

Clytemnestra (*in anger and distress*) What kind of obscenity is this that you men have plotted? You dig deep into the evil sewers of your minds and dredge up this—this—abomination.
Kalchas Madam, it is a necessity. We are driven by necessity.

Andreas and Penelope lower the trunk. During the following,

Goodbye, Iphigenia 11

Andreas is seen to whisper into Penelope's ear. As he speaks, she mimes an attempt at a scream, but Andreas stifles it with his hand over her mouth. Then he takes her into a comforting embrace, as she heaves with silent sobbing

Clytemnestra Necessity? Since when has it ever been necessary for men to pervert the common laws of Nature? If, as is so often claimed, Nature has appointed you the protectors of the female of the species, how could any necessity arise that would force you into subverting what has been thus ordained?
Kalchas You heard your husband, the King, explain.
Clytemnestra Husband? King? I heard the waffling babble of a weak and confused man. None of it made sense to me.
Kalchas Madam, you know that here is gathered the largest fleet and military force in the history of Greece—probably in the history of the whole known world. It is assembled here in order to embark upon an expedition of war with the aim of redeeming the honour of Prince Menelaus, that of his errant wife—your sister, Helen—and the honour and integrity of all the Greek states. But here we have lain at Aulis powerless to launch our punitive attack upon evil Troy. Here we have lain for week after week, month after month, and all for lack of the wind we need to fill the sails of our fleet. Without that wind we lie anchored here and rot.

Clytemnestra paces up and down, sometimes circling around Kalchas who, however, remains quite still like some immovable object at the centre of a storm, gazing steadfastly forward

Clytemnestra You men! You warriors! You heroes of Greece! I marvel that you cannot fill your sails with the hot air that issues from your mouths each time you speak. If you are so adept at puffing up your pride and prowess, how comes it that you can't puff up a few yards of sailcloth?
Kalchas Do you know, Clytemnestra, how it is when an army primed to fight, and, aye, prepared to die, is forced to stagnate for an endless time? I'll tell you how it is. There is the slow erosion

of the manly spirit, the cancer-like gnawing away of the civilised mind. Discipline disintegrates, mutiny is inspired. The lash can do so much and then no more. The noose can hold its terror but for a brief time. Anarchy takes root, then flourishes, spreading through the ranks like a viral disease, a deadly plague. Souls enthused with dreams of glory and victory feel their dreams turn sour and decay. Men keyed up for bloody acts of war begin instead to think of their unattended crops, their empty beds, their unseeded wives and sweethearts.

Clytemnestra And the obscenity you propose for my poor child will reverse all that? What kind of logic is that? Insane, brutish, bestial logic, that's what it is.

Kalchas I, as High Priest, was commissioned by Agamemnon and the general staff to discover why the winds necessary to speed us on our way to Troy were being denied us.

Clytemnestra You mean, Kalchas, that you went into one of your famous drug-induced trances.

Kalchas I liberated my mind in order to transcend the earth-bound state. My spirit soared to commune with the gods.

Clytemnestra (*derisively*) Ha!

Kalchas In the other-world I learned the truth. Upon my spirit's return to the plane of dust and clay, I reported that truth to the King and general staff.

Clytemnestra That the nose of the goddess Artemis had been put out of joint?

Kalchas Crudely put, Clytemnestra, but in essence true. Officers and soldiers, including Agamemnon himself, had been hunting profanely in woods and groves sacred to Artemis. The army had been feeding illicitly upon animal flesh that was under the protection of the goddess. In retaliation, therefore, she has stilled the wind for which our sails hunger.

Clytemnestra What rot! What superstitious mumbo-jumbo! How can the reasoning minds of civilised beings be so corrupted as to give such nonsense even the ghost of credence? Such fabrication might impress children, but it passes all understanding that grown men should let it clog their powers of reason. And then to

Goodbye, Iphigenia

suggest that the remedy to lift this trumped-up curse should lie in—in——

Kalchas Human sacrifice? What is it, madam, when a state sends an army off to war but a demand for human sacrifice, not to appease the gods but to satisfy the human lust for blood. And you, Queen Clytemnestra, no less than all the other females and the grey-headed elders, waved your handkerchief with delighted fervour, as you watched the army of young men march off to war. In your innermost heart you must have known that before any victory could be achieved, death would inevitably thin out their ranks. Yet still you cheered to see them go. You waved, you cheered, you urged them on, for to you they were faceless, nameless entities. The blood they would spill, the lives they would lay down, no more to you than dues that had to be paid to preserve the order and security and comforts of your society.

Clytemnestra How that priestly tongue of yours can twist logic, Kalchas. There is a whole world of difference between hot warfare and the cold-blooded act of taking a young girl's life with a knife upon an altar.

Kalchas Necessity motivates both things, madam.

Clytemnestra Why Iphigenia? Why *my* child? Answer me that!

Kalchas Because she is who she is. Because society is ordered in a particular way. Because she is part of the ruling class, and the ruling class can only lead by example. When I reported it had been divinely decreed a virgin sacrifice was required from the royal house, Agamemnon could have refused to surrender Iphigenia's life. He did not. What was proposed was contrary to all he is as a loving father, even as a good, kind man, but at rock-bottom he knows his claim to kingship rests upon the expectation that for the good of all his subjects he must be prepared to sacrifice what is dearest to his heart.

Clytemnestra Yes, I can see that in the heat of the moment he would agree to that. It would vaunt his ego, make him an object of amazement in other men's eyes, bestow on him the persona of an awesome hero. When it was no more than a sort of abstract proposal, I can imagine him succumbing to the allure and mystery attached to it. But now—now that it could become a reality, he surely must withdraw his consent.

Kalchas Should he do so, he would lose all respect. When it came to the crunch, it would be said, he retreated from facing up to what, as King, he demanded in the name of patriotism from lesser mortals—the sacrifice of loved ones. That sort of humiliation would destroy him and the whole royal house.

Clytemnestra But, don't you see, Iphigenia is the child he loves the best in all the world?

Kalchas Everyone knows it, and that is why this act of sacrifice by him will ring throughout the corridors of history for generations to come.

Clytemnestra I pray future generations may scorn it for the evil it is.

Kalchas That may be, but in practical terms our sights must now be concentrated upon the present generation. The army has been promised Iphigenia's blood to cleanse them of their sins and to bring about the winds that will guide us to the Trojan shores. Deny the army that blood and it will disintegrate and all the strength of Greece will drain away.

Clytemnestra And what, Kalchas, of your hidden agenda? Perhaps because I see with a mother's eyes you cannot quite conceal your personal motive from me.

Kalchas I don't know what you mean.

Clytemnestra The King and nobles command and all the rest must obey, but in the dark channels of your wily heart, Kalchas, I'll wager you're dancing a jig of triumph, singing a secret anthem of self-congratulation, for the lesson you're really driving home is that at the end of the day you rule the King and yours is the real power in the land. It is to your greed for personal power that Iphigenia is really being sacrificed. You, you devil incarnate, are behind all this horror. (*With a snarl of hate she launches an attack upon Kalchas, beating upon his chest with her fists, scratching and clawing*)

He grasps her wrists and subdues her, forcing her to her knees

Kalchas Madam, it has been said that queens should be cold and

Goodbye, Iphigenia 15

wise, and if they cannot achieve that, then they should make a good stab at faking it. Now listen to me. If you act like a common hysterical mother, a blubbering weak-minded peasant woman, then you'll undermine the whole concept of royalty. If you cannot rise above the level of personal tragedy, you will forfeit the right to wear the diadem that gives you the power to rule over the lower orders. They expect you to have a will of iron, a heart of stone. Disappoint them, and you will see the entire social structure you believe in topple to the ground.

Clytemnestra And what happens to you, Kalchas, when my child is sacrificed and still no wind will breathe into the sails of the Greek fleet?

Kalchas Madam, if, as we are taught, faith can move mountains, then surely it can cause a breeze to blow.

Clytemnestra Unhand me, priest!

Kalchas releases his hold upon Clytemnestra who draws herself up regally

So be it. But, Kalchas, in my bosom I shall always nurse my spite against you, and there will come a time when a queen's strength and a mother's hate will bring you to the dust. Even the strongest pillar of the strongest temple can be made to crumble in time.

Kalchas Amen to that, dear lady, but only if it be the will of the gods.

Agamemnon comes forward c in despondent fashion

Agamemnon For pity's sake, wife, go to our wretched child. She is beyond my comfort. Give her, as only a mother can do, the resolve to face what is inevitable.

Clytemnestra What a state this world would be in if women lacked the strength and ingenuity to unravel the muddles scheming men create. (*She goes to the* UR *area*)

Agamemnon Oh, Kalchas, this is a bitch of a business.

Kalchas Yet it must be proceeded with—and hastily. Can't you feel the electric tension shooting through the silence holding the camp in its grip? Such tension can only be kept under restraint for a very limited period. The men have sniffed the air, caught the scent of blood in their nostrils, and now strain like anxious hounds upon the leash.

Agamemnon Yes, yes, I know they must have the moment of spectacle and blood-letting they crave for, but, Kalchas—and now, you understand, I speak as one experienced in the machinations of practical politics—does it matter—I mean *really* matter—who it is that lies under the knife?

Kalchas Are you suggesting a substitute of some kind?

Agamemnon Iphigenia—so to speak—by proxy. Let us say—just by way of example—her young handmaiden. No-one would be close enough to the altar to spot the difference.

Kalchas (*thoughtfully*) It is possible such a trick might be engineered without too much difficulty, Majesty, provided the victim had been suitably subdued.

Agamemnon Yes, exactly, Kalchas. Just a matter of careful manipulation.

Kalchas Of course, the cover-up would be enormously complicated. That Iphigenia continued to live would somehow have to be concealed from the public for the rest of her natural life.

Agamemnon That wouldn't be beyond our ingenuity.

Kalchas The danger of revelation would stalk us all forever.

Agamemnon It would be a risk worth taking.

Kalchas It is a dire thing to deceive the whole nation.

Agamemnon It's been done before with even less justification, Kalchas.

Kalchas True.

Agamemnon So you agree?

Kalchas (*after a pause and then very matter-of-factly*) No, of course not, Majesty. In certain circumstances I might agree to deceive the rabble, but I would not ever dare to deceive the gods. Why, that would be utterly sacrilegious, and I am surprised, Majesty, you should ask such a thing of the High Priest. Quite out of the question. Now, time wears on and arrangements have to be put under way.

Agamemnon (*crestfallen*) For a moment there I thought—I hoped—my child might yet be saved.

Goodbye, Iphigenia 17

Kalchas Put that sort of foolishness out of your head. (*He raises his voice*) You, girl!

Penelope disengages from Andreas and looks at Kalchas questioningly. She points to herself

Yes, you. Come here.

Penelope hesitatingly crosses C. *She gives low obeisance to Agamemnon*

Penelope Oh, Majesty, say it isn't true what's to happen to my lady.
Agamemnon I wish I could give you the assurance you ask.
Kalchas No doubt, my girl, you're worried about being out of a place after today, but, let me tell you, Fate might have faced you with a much worse prospect than mere unemployment. (*To Agamemnon*) Isn't that so, sir? (*To Penelope*) However, until you are redundant as a maid-servant, you must do your duty towards the princess as conscientiously as ever. Come, follow me, girl, to my tent.
Penelope (*doubtfully*) To your tent, reverend?
Kalchas Yes, girl, to my tent. Now, come.

Kalchas, followed by Penelope, exits L

Andreas adopts his sentry pose as Agamemnon buries his face in outspread hands

Agamemnon (*removing his hands from his face*) Sentry! Sentry, come here!

Andreas stamps his way C *and with much sword flourishing salutes Agamemnon*

Andreas Majesty, sentry Andreas reporting as commanded. Sir!
Agamemnon Put up your sword, my man.
Andreas (*sheathing the sword and stamping some more*) Sir!

Agamemnon Oh, forget all that military stuff for a moment, young fellow. I want us to speak together man-to-man.
Andreas (*obviously confused*) Speak, sir? Me? Me—speak to your Majesty?
Agamemnon Without restraint upon your tongue. Honestly and frankly. Tell me, when you look upon me what do you see?
Andreas See, sir? Well, I suppose I see the King. Yes, if it please your Majesty, I see the King.
Agamemnon Is that all?
Andreas (*cautiously, as if fearful of being found wanting*) Not all, sir. No, not all.
Agamemnon Well?
Andreas I see the Commander-in-Chief o' this great army.
Agamemnon And is that all?
Andreas Good 'eavens, no, sir. A long way from being all, sir.
Agamemnon Go on then.
Andreas Um—let me see, sir. I see—I see—there's such a lot, sir. Ah, yes, I see a person o' great breeding, a man o' destiny, a man who 'as power and brains and wealth and—and—and—
Agamemnon But basically still a man?
Andreas A man, sir? W-e-ll, not exactly, sir. More o' a real gent, sir; a first-rate toff, sir; a—a—proper nobleman, sir.
Agamemnon Don't you see a father?
Andreas A father, sir?
Agamemnon Yes. A man who has sired children.
Andreas Oh, I know that, sir. Everyone knows *that*, sir.
Agamemnon And what do you think of a father who would kill his own child?
Andreas That 'e ain't natural. I'd string up any such bastards 'as go in for that sort o' thing, sir. Begging your pardon, sir, and not wishing to tell you your job nor nothing, I think you should make a law against such perverts, sir.
Agamemnon So you see me as a pervert?
Andreas No, sir, not *you*. I meant unnatural fathers, sir. Them wot abuse their children.
Agamemnon Yet I have agreed my daughter should be submitted to the knife.

Goodbye, Iphigenia 19

Andreas But that's different, sir. That ain't wot you'd call your actual abuse, sir.
Agamemnon Why not?
Andreas Because—because—well, it's part o' the war effort, ain't it, sir?
Agamemnon An innocent girl has to die for the war effort, is that it?
Andreas It's 'ard lines and all that, sir, but it's like wot we is all told: everyone must do 'is and 'er duty for the good o' the state, specially in time o' war. There ain't no 'elp for that, sir. In the name o' our one true religion, our king, and our country, we got to be willing to sacrifice everything we is.
Agamemnon You have been well versed in the lesson.
Andreas Thank you, sir. Very kind o' you, I'm sure, sir.
Agamemnon Very well, you may return to your duty, soldier.
Andreas (*unsheathing the sword, stamping feet, making a flourishing sword salute*) Yes, sir. (*Hesitatingly*) If I might say so, Majesty, it's been a great honour for a 'umble bloke like me to 'ave 'ad this chat with you. You're a real hero and king, and I pray the gods will long look over you and bless you. (*He returns to formality and feet stamping*) Sir! (*He about turns and returns to his place* R)

Agamemnon again buries his face in his hands. When he speaks, he could be weeping, or he might be laughing

Agamemnon Oh, blessed heaven, they haven't the foggiest of what any of it is about. (*He remains with his face in his hands*)

Penelope enters L. *She carries a small bottle. She passes quickly by Agamemnon, bobbing him a curtsy. When she reaches* R *she encounters Andreas*

Andreas (*out of the side of his mouth*) Wot's that bottle you got there, Penelope girl?
Penelope It was given me by the High Priest. He said as how I must tell the Queen that the princess has got to drink up every last drop.

Andreas Wot is it, then?
Penelope I don't know, do I? Some kind of medicine, I reckon. Something for her poor nerves, I shouldn't wonder.
Andreas A drop o' the 'ard stuff, I daresay, or some sort o' drug that'll blow 'er mind clean up to the clouds, poor cow.
Penelope I'd best take it in, although how I'm going to face my lady I just don't know. My legs are like jelly, and that's no lie.

Penelope enters the UR *area which is now lit. Iphigenia is sitting upon the couch, curled up, her face turned away from the audience and buried in the upholstery of the couch, as if she seeks to hide. From the heaving of her body it is obvious that she is deeply distressed. Clytemnestra stands behind the couch looking down at Iphigenia, one hand stretched out, as if to offer comfort, but the hand hovers rather than actually touching Iphigenia's body*

Iphigenia (*in a muffled, sobbing voice*) But why me, Mother? I haven't done anything wrong. Why should they want to punish me?
Clytemnestra Of course you've not done anything wrong, and it isn't punishment, my child.
Iphigenia But death is how they punish traitors and murderers. Death is for bad people, Mother, and I'm not bad. Oh, please, for pity's sake, Mother, tell them I'm not bad. Tell them I don't deserve to die. Mother, as you love me, beg them to spare me. I'm afraid, so terribly afraid. I've never been so afraid before in my whole life.
Clytemnestra I would crawl a hundred miles on my hands and knees, my darling, if it would do any good, but they are quite adamant. They have hardened their hearts. They've done so in the name of duty, and it is as a hard duty that they require you to accept this bitter fate.
Iphigenia It is the dark I fear the most, Mother. It's the dark and coldness of the grave that fills me with such awful dread and horror.
Clytemnestra There will be neither dark nor cold for you, my daughter. You will sleep and then awake to the golden light and

warmth of that place where it is said the gods all dwell. You will be embraced by them and garlanded with immortality.

Penelope begins silently weeping

Iphigenia I don't want to dwell with gods. I want to live among real people. I want to have all the years of living I was looking forward to. I want to be happy here on earth. I don't want to die, not for duty or any other reason.
Clytemnestra (*to Penelope*) What are you about, girl?
Penelope (*drying her eyes*) If it please you, ma'am, his reverence the High Priest says the princess must drink every drop of this. (*She extends the bottle to Clytemnestra*)

Clytemnestra takes it and examines it

Clytemnestra What is it?
Penelope I don't know, ma'am, but he said——
Clytemnestra (*interrupting*) Yes, yes, all right. Now, go to the trunk and bring out the bridal gown. And bring me my scarlet scarf.
Penelope Oh, ma'am, there's surely something that can be done to stop all this. It isn't right such a thing should happen. It really isn't.
Clytemnestra Tell that to the men, and see if they will listen to you! Even if you could persuade them it was a vile and monstrous thing, you would find they are such prisoners of their indoctrination they would not have the power to lift as much as one little finger to stop it. Each and every one of us is an integral part of the juggernaut which is the philosophy of our nation, and when the machine grinds into motion there is no braking system we may apply to halt its relentless drive. And we poor things must reconcile ourselves to being carried forward with it, even if it lumbers on into the abyss.
Penelope I don't understand, Majesty, I truly don't.
Clytemnestra Non-understanding is what the machine demands of us. Go, girl and do as I have bid you. Attending to little duties and

adhering to the petty routines of normality may help to blunt the pain of not understanding.
Penelope If you say so, ma'am.

As Penelope leaves the UR *area it is plunged into darkness. She goes to where the trunk is situated. She kneels and opens the trunk's lid*

Andreas (*observing her*) 'Ow's she doing?
Penelope My lady? How would you expect? Beside herself, of course. She can't fathom it at all, poor child. Nor can anyone else, as far as I can see. It's like finding yourself locked up in the mental asylum with all the crazy people.
Andreas Women don't understand them things. Not your fault— it's 'ow you're made. You're not trained in deep things, complicated things, see. It takes a man to 'andle such things.
Penelope You just shut your mouth, you great heartless oaf, before I knock your block off. I mean it, I really do!
Andreas (*laughing*) That's all right, Penelope darling, I know that's just your 'igh-strung nerves speaking. I don't take offence.

Kalchas enters L *and approaches Agamemnon* C

Agamemnon removes his hands from his face. Kalchas guides Agamemnon into turning around and together they walk up stage towards the area of the altar which is now lit. The two men stand before the altar and Kalchas is seen to be speaking to Agamemnon

During the following, Penelope withdraws from the trunk a white gown and a red silk scarf, which should be large enough to later cover the face and upper body part of Iphigenia

Kalchas makes hand gestures, as if indicating silently where and how a body would be laid upon the altar. He then removes from his robes a dagger. He raises it in both hands high above his head, and then plunges it down towards the altar. Having done so, he hands the dagger to Agamemnon and with a gesture of his hand indicates that Agamemnon should carry out the actions he has just illustrated.

Goodbye, Iphigenia

Agamemnon looks puzzled, but then, as comprehension dawns upon him, he violently mimes his refusal. He tries unsuccessfully to pass the dagger back to Kalchas

Penelope closes the trunk lid and, carrying the gown and scarf, she enters the unlit UR *area*

Iphigenia *(screaming)* No, no, I will not wear that shroud! Mother, don't make me wear it, please!
Clytemnestra My child, it must be. It's what will be expected. Penelope, come help me dress the princess.

Up stage, Agamemnon in a show of revulsion throws the dagger down on to the stage. He turns and rushes C. *Kalchas stoops to pick up the dagger and then follows Agamemnon* C

Agamemnon No, no, a thousand times no, Kalchas. That was never part of the bargain.
Kalchas The bargain was that you would sacrifice your child.
Agamemnon Submit her to sacrifice, aye, but not to do the deed myself. It would be unnatural and unthinkable.
Kalchas Yes, for lesser men. But it is imperative that your hand be seen to be the one that does it. That is what will mark you out from all other mortals.
Agamemnon I am her father. It was my seed that called her into life.
Kalchas Who else then has better right to terminate that life?
Agamemnon Between giving the word of consent and the implementation of the act there is a whole ocean of difference. I will not embark upon that ocean.
Kalchas You must.
Agamemnon Never!
Kalchas You must! *(Cajolingly)* I know, Majesty, how terrible a thing it is to contemplate, but I shall be at your side. My spiritual strength will be there for you to lean upon, but it is your kingly strength that must perform the act. Afterwards men will say of you: "Here was a man like no other. Here was one who could

translate the unthinkable into action". Your name will be revered. Your life will be held up throughout the history of men as an example of awesome uniqueness. You will have earned the status of a god.

Agamemnon If they but knew the truth, Kalchas.

Kalchas The truth is what must never be revealed to them. The truth must stay hidden inside of you. The only truth men will be able to testify to is what they've witnessed with their eyes. They need see no deeper than that. The image alone is paramount.

Agamemnon This will be the death of me.

Iphigenia comes running from out of the darkness of the UR area, dressed in the white gown, and falls to a crouching position. She stays upon her hands and knees on the stage. She makes grating, howling sounds like a wounded animal. Clytemnestra and Penelope quickly follow her. Together they attempt to raise her up, but she scrabbles about on the stage, resisting them. Clytemnestra holds the small bottle in one hand. Penelope is in a state of distress. Agamemnon and Kalchas watch the scene—Agamemnon with horror, Kalchas with something like distaste

Clytemnestra (*on the floor, attempting to direct the bottle towards Iphigenia's lips*) Drink this, my pet, and everything will be all right.

Iphigenia (*resisting*) No, no, take it away! You want to murder me. You all want to murder me.

Penelope (*to Clytemnestra*) Oh, ma'am, I cannot bear this.

Clytemnestra (*to Penelope*) Hold her, girl, until I get this potion down her throat.

Penelope Ma'am, forgive me, but I can't bring myself to do that to my sweet lady.

Clytemnestra It's your duty to do it, you silly female. Don't you see, it will bring blessed unconsciousness to her poor distraught mind. (*To Iphigenia*) Drink it, darling, like a good girl. Drink it for Mother's sake.

Iphigenia still howls, still resists

Goodbye, Iphigenia

(*To Penelope*) Hold her, girl, hold her!
Penelope (*backing away, whimpering*) I can't, I can't.
Clytemnestra (*to Andreas*) Soldier, help me.
Andreas Yes, Majesty. (*He kneels on the stage behind Iphigenia, pulls her back against his body, puts his arms tightly around her, imprisoning her arms. In a soothing voice*) There, there, my sweet little lady, be calm, be peaceful, and everything will come right, you'll see. I 'ave you safe in my arms. No-one can't 'urt you now, little princess. Andreas 'as you all nice and safe.
Iphigenia (*quietly*) Nice and safe?
Andreas That's right. No-one can 'arm you, my precious lady, as long as Andreas 'olds you safe.
Iphigenia Yes, yes, hold me safe. Promise to keep me safe.
Andreas I will and all, little beauty. I will. (*To Clytemnestra*) Now, ma'am, now!

Clytemnestra puts the bottle to Iphigenia's lips

Clytemnestra Drink, my darling, and you'll feel so much better.
Iphigenia I don't want to, Mother.
Andreas You drink up like the good girl you is, and you'll feel all nice and peaceful.

Iphigenia relents and drinks

That's the way, little princess. (*He laughs gently*) Oh, oh, who's dribbling then? Mustn't waste the nice stuff that'll make you all better. (*Gently rocking his body*) There, see, all done, and now you won't 'ave no nasty nerves troubling you no more.
Clytemnestra She has relaxed now, soldier. You may let the princess go.
Andreas Yes, ma'am. (*He releases Iphigenia from his embrace. He rises to his feet and stamps to attention*) Will that be all, Majesty?

Clytemnestra raises a now docile Iphigenia into an upright position

Clytemnestra (*to Andreas*) Yes, you may go, soldier.
Andreas (*in a barking military voice*) Yes, Majesty. (*With stamping feet he returns to his former place*)

Clytemnestra, supporting Iphigenia, moves back into the darkened UR *area, and Penelope quietly follows them. Agamemnon and Kalchas observe the females go*

Agamemnon That my daughter should be reduced to that pitiful state!
Kalchas Yes, sire, it was, unfortunately, a shade unseemly.
Agamemnon She who had shown such promise of developing real regal dignity! She's the patroness of the Ladies' Association of Fine Thread Spinners, you know, and carried out her duties with marvellous decorum and presence. Quite delighted everyone. And when she made appearance in the royal box at the annual games she fairly stole the hearts of the populace. Everyone remarked upon how she bore herself with commendable grace and charm. Then when she visited the veterans' hospital——
Kalchas (*interrupting*) Yes, Majesty, a credit to her parents and the nation, I'm sure. That sort of thing, however, must be consigned to memory, for a more pressing duty now demands to be acted out. (*He points* L) See, sir, the army is being drawn up in formation.
Agamemnon What! Is the fateful hour come upon us already?
Kalchas It has to be over and done with before the setting of the sun. We don't want the solemnity of the ritual to be spoiled by fading light.

There is a sound of trumpets off stage

Agamemnon How my hands shake and my legs tremble!
Kalchas Take a grip upon yourself, sire. The ceremony requires you to be fully in control. (*He calls out to Andreas*) Soldier, inform the Queen we are ready to commence.

Andreas stamps to the UR *area*

Goodbye, Iphigenia 27

Andreas Majesty, 'is reverence the 'igh priest presents 'is compliments and says it is time to begin. (*He stands a little to the side*)

Out of the darkness comes Clytemnestra supporting Iphigenia, while Penelope, sobbing quietly, head downcast, comes behind carrying the red scarf

Iphigenia (*in a childish, slurred voice*) Oh, look, Mother darling, it's the kind young soldier who's promised to keep me nice and safe.
Clytemnestra That's right, my dear. Now, head up, back straight, and walk with dignity, just as you've always been taught to do.
Iphigenia (*giggling*) My head's so woozy I can hardly feel my feet touching the ground. Hold on to me or else—(*she laughs almost uproariously*) or else, Mother, I'll float quite away.

They walk towards C, followed by Penelope, and Andreas takes up the rear. When they reach Agamemnon and Kalchas, they come to a halt. Kalchas conceals the knife in his robes

(*Still giggling*) Father, I'm all sort of floaty. I think I'm turning into a feather. Isn't that strange and funny?
Agamemnon Oh, my own dear child.

The sound of trumpets offstage. As the trumpet sounds die, they are replaced by the measured beat of a drum

Iphigenia (*bubbling over with laughter*) How solemn that drum is. Dum-dum-dum. It isn't in the least good music to float to. Don't you think we should have something more lively, Father? Stringed instruments would be ever so much more jolly. You can't sing out whee-ee-ee to something as turgid as dum-dum-dum. (*She breaks free from Clytemnestra and with outstretched arms gyrates wildly, laughing all the while*)
Agamemnon Clytemnestra, can't you still her chatter and stop her hysteria? It wounds me so deeply to see her like this.

Clytemnestra Between Kalchas and yourself you have contrived to create a tragedy that now disintegrates into a farce. Don't ask me, therefore, to salvage any shred of dignity from the unholy mess.
Kalchas No squabbling, please, in front of the army. It ruins the image.

Agamemnon restrains Iphigenia, putting his arm around her waist

Agamemnon Come, my dear, you must walk nicely beside Father.
Iphigenia Are we going to float up the aisle together, Daddy?
Kalchas Let us proceed . I'll walk in front. You, Agamemnon, follow with the princess. The Queen will walk behind you. (*He begins to walk up stage*)

Agamemnon follows, still holding Iphigenia. Clytemnestra takes the scarf from Penelope and then walks behind Agamemnon and Iphigenia. Andreas and Penelope draw back to stand DR. *The drum beat continues*

Iphigenia To whom did you say I am to be married, Father? (*She laughs*) Isn't it ridiculous—I quite forget. Is he young? Is he beautiful? Oh, Daddy, most of all—will he be gentle? I truly want to give my virginity to a husband, but I do rather fear there might he physical pain. (*She looks back at Clytemnestra*) Will there be much blood, Mother?
Agamemnon Hush, my lamb, we are now at the holy altar.

Kalchas turns and he and Agamemnon lift up Iphigenia to lay her upon the altar

Iphigenia I feel quite drowsy now. In fact, I think perhaps I'm already asleep and dreaming.

Kalchas and Agamemnon stand side by side, Clytemnestra behind them. Iphigenia is mostly concealed from the audience. Kalchas raises both arms in the air

Goodbye, Iphigenia

Kalchas (*in a loud intoning voice*) Because men are sinful and disobedient creatures who would defile the world they inhabit, the gods must sit in judgment upon them, for the gods alone have the power to bring headstrong humanity to heel and to direct wayward feet on to the path of righteousness. Without the gods there would be neither reason nor purpose. Only by complying with the moral demands made by the gods through the agency of our earthly church can there be achieved survival and order. In the wisdom of the gods alone can we find hope and refuge. When frail Man errs he must make humble plea for pardon, submit himself meekly to trial, and in a spirit of contrite acceptance endure the sentence passed. By the grace of the gods, the blood of one innocent can wash clean the guilt of the many. In that great mystery, far beyond the comprehension of ordinary men, lies the joy of salvation. When the gods command, we must obey. (*He lowers his arms*)

The offstage drum breaks its beat and then goes into a fast roll. From his robes, Kalchas withdraws the knife. He hands it to Agamemnon. Agamemnon appears reluctant to accept it, but Kalchas forces it upon him. Agamemnon gives voice to a long groan. He raises the knife high into the air in both his hands

Iphigenia (*in a frightened childish voice*) Don't, Daddy, please, don't! I'll be good, I promise. Please, Daddy, don't!
Kalchas Now, man, now!

Agamemnon screams and plunges the knife downwards. The drumming ceases abruptly. Agamemnon lets the knife fall to the ground. Off stage there is the sound of unified male sighing. Then there is the sound of bird wings fluttering. Penelope takes a step forward, pointing upwards

Penelope Oh, the gods be praised, look! My lady's soul has turned into a dove and flies up to heaven. She lives! She lives!

The sound of male cheering off stage. Clytemnestra steps forward to the altar and drapes Iphigenia with the scarlet scarf

Clytemnestra Is everyone happy now?

Agamemnon and Kalchas turn away from the altar. Clytemnestra walks behind them, and they move towards the UR area. At the entrance to the tent interior, Kalchas stops and looks around

Kalchas (*exultingly*) Can you feel it? There is a breeze got up. The gods have sent us wind for our sails. Now, come the dawn, we are fair set for Troy and a righteous war.

More male cheering off stage

Black-out

All except Andreas exit

The Lights come up DC and Andreas stands alone, once more hooded and enveloped in his cloak

Andreas (*in his old man's voice*) That's the way it were. Leastways, that's the way I remember it, and 'ow else do dead souls survive 'cept in the memory o' the living. Poor young cow, 'er death certainly seemed to bring us the wind we needed to get to 'ell out o' bleeding Aulis. A desperate kind o' way to earn a breeze, if you ask me. I'll tell you something, and you can laugh if you want to, but many a man who were there that day at Aulis admitted later round the camp fires at Troy that when the knife went into Iphigenia they—well, you know—they 'ad a sudden moment o' sexual relief. Sort o' involuntary relief, if you know wot I mean. Queer thing that, ain't it? I'll tell you something else, too: that lass Penelope come through the tent lines that night and sought me out, she did. And the pair o' us went into a dark place and went at it like knives. There weren't no love about it, none o' wot you'd call your romantic passion. It were just two people trying to blank out from their minds wot 'ad 'appened that day. Seeking comfort like two dumb animals, you might say. Never saw 'er again after that. She's probably a grandma now if she's still alive upon the face o' the earth. Poor bitch, she really believed Iphigenia's soul went off to 'eaven as a dove. Me, I think it were no more than a pigeon frightened out o' the undergrowth by all the noise. Still, it were a long time afore I ever really relished pigeon pie again. During that awful bloody war at Troy, us soldiers often talked o' the Princess Iphigenia and wot 'appened at Aulis. We 'ad this song we used to march to. (*He painfully marks time, and in his tuneless, cracked voice he sings*)

> Goodbye, Iphigenia,
> We owe an awful lot to you.
> You took our sins upon your lovely 'ead,
> You took the knife, and now you're blinking dead.
> Goodbye, Iphigenia,
> You'll never 'ave a pretty lover boy,
> But we'll recall your name, by thunder,
> As we rape and as we plunder,
> Us lads wot fight the war in Troy.

(*He laughs*) "Don't give us none o' that ancient 'istory, Dad," the young ones say, but me, I say, I'm Private Andreas, veteran o' the Trojan war, and bloody proud o' it, too. Ancient 'istory? I bloody well *am* ancient 'istory, and I'm still alive and kicking. So stuff the young ones, says I. (*He laughs again, turns away and slowly shuffles* L)

Black-out

FURNITURE AND PROPERTY LIST

Further dressing may be added at the director's discretion

On stage: Couch
Carpets
Hangings arranged as interior of a tent
Altar-shaped structure draped overall in black material

Off stage: Trunk containing white gown and red silk scarf (**Andreas** and **Penelope**)
Small bottle (**Penelope**)

Personal: **Andreas:** sheathed sword
Kalchas: dagger

LIGHTING PLOT

Property fittings required: nil
1 interior/exterior setting. The same throughout. Two concentrated areas of light—UR and UC

To open: Lights on DC

Cue 1	**Andreas** moves UR *Bring up lighting on* UR *area*	(Page 2)
Cue 2	**All** reach the tent interior *Fade out lighting on* UR *area*	(Page 8)
Cue 3	**Penelope** enters UR area *Bring up lighting on* UR *area*	(Page 20)
Cue 4	**Penelope** leaves UR area *Black-out on* UR *area*	(Page 22)
Cue 5	**Kalchas** and **Agamemnon** walk towards altar *Bring up lighting on altar* UC	(Page 22)
Cue 6	Male cheering off stage *Black-out*	(Page 30)
Cue 7	**All** except **Andreas** exit *Bring up lighting on* **Andreas** DC	(Page 30)
Cue 8	**Andreas** shuffles L *Black-out*	(Page 31)

EFFECTS PLOT

Cue 1	**Kalchas**: "…and personal vulnerability." *Trumpet fanfares off stage, merging with cacophony of male voices cheering and shouting*	(Page 6)
Cue 2	**Kalchas**: "…spoiled by fading light." *Trumpets off stage*	(Page 26)
Cue 3	**Agamemnon**: "Oh, my own dear child." *Trumpets off stage, then replaced by measured beat of drum, continuing*	(Page 27)
Cue 4	**Kalchas** lowers his arms *Drum beat breaks, then goes into a fast roll*	(Page 29)
Cue 5	**Agamemnon** plunges the knife downwards *Cut drumming*	(Page 29)
Cue 6	**Agamemnon** lets the knife fall to the ground *Unified male sighing off stage, then the sound of bird wings fluttering*	(Page 29)
Cue 7	**Penelope**: "She lives!" *Male cheering off stage*	(Page 29)
Cue 8	**Kalchas**: "… a righteous war." *More male cheering off stage*	(Page 30)

www.ingramcontent.com/pod-product-compliance
Lightning Source LLC
Chambersburg PA
CBHW070454050426
42450CB00012B/3267